SPRINKLE
YOUR
Thoughts

Sprinkle Your Thoughts is your space to let it all out—dreams, reflections, lists, or doodles. However you choose to use it, these pages are yours to sprinkle with whatever's on your mind and heart.

Sprinkle Your Thoughts

Sprinkle Your Thoughts

Sprinkle Your Thoughts

Sprinkle Your Thoughts

Sprinkle Your Thoughts

Sprinkle Your Thoughts

Sprinkle Your Thoughts

Sprinkle Your Thoughts

Sprinkle Your Thoughts

Sprinkle Your Thoughts

Sprinkle Your Thoughts

Sprinkle Your Thoughts

_____

_____

_____

_____

_____

_____

_____

_____

_____

_____

_____

_____

_____

_____

_____

_____

_____

_____

_____

_____

_____

Sprinkle Your Thoughts

Sprinkle Your Thoughts

Sprinkle Your Thoughts

Sprinkle Your Thoughts

Sprinkle Your Thoughts

Sprinkle Your Thoughts

Sprinkle Your Thoughts

Sprinkle Your Thoughts

_____

_____

_____

_____

_____

_____

_____

_____

_____

_____

_____

_____

_____

_____

_____

_____

_____

_____

_____

Sprinkle Your Thoughts

Sprinkle Your Thoughts

Sprinkle Your Thoughts

Sprinkle Your Thoughts

Sprinkle Your Thoughts

Sprinkle Your Thoughts

Sprinkle Your Thoughts

_____

_____

_____

_____

_____

_____

_____

_____

_____

_____

_____

_____

_____

_____

_____

_____

_____

_____

_____

_____

_____

Sprinkle Your Thoughts

Sprinkle Your Thoughts

Sprinkle Your Thoughts

Sprinkle Your Thoughts

Sprinkle Your Thoughts

Sprinkle Your Thoughts

Sprinkle Your Thoughts

Sprinkle Your Thoughts

Sprinkle Your Thoughts

Sprinkle Your Thoughts

_____

_____

_____

_____

_____

_____

_____

_____

_____

_____

_____

_____

_____

_____

_____

_____

_____

_____

_____

_____

Sprinkle Your Thoughts

Sprinkle Your Thoughts

Sprinkle Your Thoughts

Sprinkle Your Thoughts

Sprinkle Your Thoughts

Sprinkle Your Thoughts

Sprinkle Your Thoughts

Sprinkle Your Thoughts

Sprinkle Your Thoughts

Sprinkle Your Thoughts

Sprinkle Your Thoughts

Sprinkle Your Thoughts

Sprinkle Your Thoughts

Sprinkle Your Thoughts

Sprinkle Your Thoughts

Sprinkle Your Thoughts

Sprinkle Your Thoughts

Sprinkle Your Thoughts

Sprinkle Your Thoughts

Sprinkle Your Thoughts

Sprinkle Your Thoughts

Sprinkle Your Thoughts

Sprinkle Your Thoughts

Sprinkle Your Thoughts

Sprinkle Your Thoughts

Sprinkle Your Thoughts

Sprinkle Your Thoughts

Sprinkle Your Thoughts

Sprinkle Your Thoughts

Sprinkle Your Thoughts

Sprinkle Your Thoughts

Sprinkle Your Thoughts

Sprinkle Your Thoughts

Sprinkle Your Thoughts

Sprinkle Your Thoughts

Sprinkle Your Thoughts

Sprinkle Your Thoughts

Sprinkle Your Thoughts

Sprinkle Your Thoughts

Sprinkle Your Thoughts

Sprinkle Your Thoughts

Sprinkle Your Thoughts

Sprinkle Your Thoughts

_____

_____

_____

_____

_____

_____

_____

_____

_____

_____

_____

_____

_____

_____

_____

_____

_____

_____

_____

_____

_____

Sprinkle Your Thoughts

Sprinkle Your Thoughts

Sprinkle Your Thoughts

Sprinkle Your Thoughts

Sprinkle Your Thoughts

Sprinkle Your Thoughts

Sprinkle Your Thoughts

Sprinkle Your Thoughts

Sprinkle Your Thoughts

Sprinkle Your Thoughts

Sprinkle Your Thoughts

Sprinkle Your Thoughts

Sprinkle Your Thoughts

Sprinkle Your Thoughts

Sprinkle Your Thoughts

Sprinkle Your Thoughts

Sprinkle Your Thoughts

Sprinkle Your Thoughts

Sprinkle Your Thoughts

Sprinkle Your Thoughts

Sprinkle Your Thoughts

Sprinkle Your Thoughts

Sprinkle Your Thoughts

Sprinkle Your Thoughts

Sprinkle Your Thoughts

Sprinkle Your Thoughts

Sprinkle Your Thoughts

Sprinkle Your Thoughts

Sprinkle Your Thoughts

Sprinkle Your Thoughts

Sprinkle Your Thoughts

Sprinkle Your Thoughts

Sprinkle Your Thoughts

Sprinkle Your Thoughts

Sprinkle Your Thoughts

Sprinkle Your Thoughts

Sprinkle Your Thoughts

Sprinkle Your Thoughts

Sprinkle Your Thoughts

Sprinkle Your Thoughts

_____

_____

_____

_____

_____

_____

_____

_____

_____

_____

_____

_____

_____

_____

_____

_____

_____

_____

_____

Sprinkle Your Thoughts

Sprinkle Your Thoughts

Sprinkle Your Thoughts

Sprinkle Your Thoughts

Sprinkle Your Thoughts

Sprinkle Your Thoughts

Sprinkle Your Thoughts

Sprinkle Your Thoughts

Sprinkle Your Thoughts

Sprinkle Your Thoughts

Sprinkle Your Thoughts

Sprinkle Your Thoughts

Sprinkle Your Thoughts

Sprinkle Your Thoughts

Sprinkle Your Thoughts

Sprinkle Your Thoughts

Sprinkle Your Thoughts

Sprinkle Your Thoughts

Sprinkle Your Thoughts

Sprinkle Your Thoughts

Sprinkle Your Thoughts

Sprinkle Your Thoughts

Sprinkle Your Thoughts

Sprinkle Your Thoughts

Sprinkle Your Thoughts

Sprinkle Your Thoughts

Sprinkle Your Thoughts

Sprinkle Your Thoughts

Sprinkle Your Thoughts

Sprinkle Your Thoughts

Sprinkle Your Thoughts

Sprinkle Your Thoughts

Sprinkle Your Thoughts

Sprinkle Your Thoughts

Sprinkle Your Thoughts

Sprinkle Your Thoughts

_____

_____

_____

_____

_____

_____

_____

_____

_____

_____

_____

_____

_____

_____

_____

_____

_____

_____

_____

_____

Sprinkle Your Thoughts

Sprinkle Your Thoughts

Sprinkle Your Thoughts

Sprinkle Your Thoughts

Sprinkle Your Thoughts

Sprinkle Your Thoughts

Sprinkle Your Thoughts

Sprinkle Your Thoughts

Sprinkle Your Thoughts

Sprinkle Your Thoughts